Bumblebee 4

Textbook

Schroedel®

Contents

The Bumblebee song

C   G   F   C

Learn - ing Eng - lish with Bum - ble-bee at school, when

G⁷   C   Am   G

days are hot, when days are cold, with Bum - ble-bee at school.

C   G   F   C

Speak - ing, read - ing, writ - ing let - ters too, oh

beliebig oft wiederholen

G⁷   C   Am   G

would - n't it be nice to have no - thing else to do, but

Schluss

G⁷   C   G⁷   C

would - n't it be nice to have no - thing else to do.

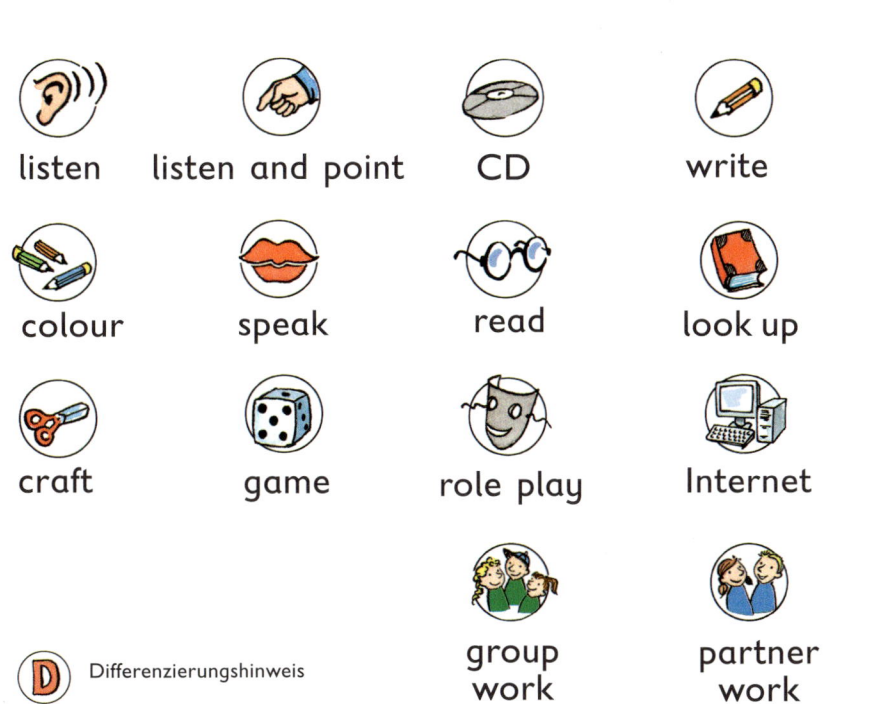

listen   listen and point   CD   write

colour   speak   read   look up

craft   game   role play   Internet

group work   partner work

(D) Differenzierungshinweis

Ein Lied gemeinsam singen.
Orientierungshilfen im Buch verstehen.

Friends around Europe

Hi, I'm Antje.
I'm ten years old.
I live in the Netherlands.
My hobbies are face painting
and sailing.

Hello, my name is Connor.
I'm nine.
I come from Great Britain.
I like surfing the Internet
and climbing.

Hello, my name is Marie.
I'm eight. I'm from France.
My hobby is painting.

(Map of Europe with labels:)

Norwegian Sea

Faeroe Islands (Den.)

Shetland Islands (U.K.)

Orkney Islands (U.K.)

Sweden

Norway

Oslo

Stoc

Denmark

Copenhagen

North Sea

Ireland

Dublin

United

Kingdom

London

Amsterdam

Netherlands

Brussels

Belgium

Lux.
Lux.

Berlin

Germany

Pragu
Czech

Channel Islands (U.K.)

Paris

France

Bern

Switzerland

Vien

Austria

Slovenia
Ljubljana

Croatia

San Marino

B
He

Monaco

Italy

Rome

Portugal

Lisbon

Madrid

Andorra

Corsica

Spain

Balearic Islands

Sardinia

Sicily

Mediter

Valletta

Malta

Algeria

Tunesia

km

Atlantic

AMSTERDAM

 1. Listen and point. Where are the children from?

 2. What do the children like?

Ländernamen und Hobbys kennenlernen.

Finland

Helsinki

Russia

Tallinn
Estonia

Riga **Latvia**

Moscow

Lithuania
to Russia Vilnius

ltic
Sea

Minsk

Belarus

Kazakhstan

Warsaw

Poland

Kiev

Ukraine

Slovakia
ratislava

Budapest

Hungary

Moldova
Kishinev

Romania

eb

Belgrade

Bucharest

Serbia and Montenegro

Sofia

Bulgaria

Skopje

Macedonia

Tirane

Albania

Greece

Athens

Crete

Georgia

Azerbaijan

Armenia

Black Sea

Iran

Ankara

Turkey

Nicosia

Cyprus

Lebanon

Sy

Ir

n e a n S e a

> Hi, I'm Mikkel.
> I'm ten years old.
> I'm from Denmark.
> My favourite hobby
> is cycling.

> Hello, I'm Sophia.
> I'm nine. I live in Poland.
> I like collecting football stickers
> and playing with my friends.

> Hi, my name is Miroslav.
> I'm eight years old.
> I come from the Czech Republic.
> My hobbies are playing the violin
> and swimming.

five

Get a penfriend!

Hi girls! Hi boys!
I'm Anna from Essen.
I'm looking for a penfriend.
My hobbies are dancing,
painting and playing chess.
What are your hobbies?
Would you like to send me
an e-mail in English?
Love,
Anna

 1. Read the text.

 2. What are Anna's hobbies?
What are your hobbies?

 3. Write an e-mail.

Hello, my name is Paul.
I'm nine years old.
I live in Berlin.
My hobby is reading.

Einen Text lesen und verstehen.
D Über Annas und über die eigenen Hobbys sprechen.

from: Ian   to: Anna
subject: Hello Anna!   cc:

Hello Anna,
thank you for your e-mail.
I come from Ireland.
My favourite hobbies are hurling, rugby and surfing the Internet.
I have a dog. His name is Shane. He is an Irish Setter.
He can do lots of tricks.
My country is famous for its coasts, sheep and hurling.
Have a look – I've sent you some photos.
Please answer soon.
Take care,
Ian

1. Read the text and find the matching pictures.

2. What is Ian's country famous for? What is your country famous for?

Einen Text lesen und verstehen.
Über Besonderheiten von Irland und dem eigenen Heimatland sprechen.

seven   7

Helping a friend

 1. Listen to the dialogue.

 2. Make a role play.

Sometimes

Sometimes I'm happy
and sometimes I'm sad.
Sometimes I'm angry
and sometimes I'm glad.
Sometimes I'm naughty
and sometimes I'm cool.
Sometimes I'm crazy and lazy at school.

Come on, come on, let's say it again:
sometimes we're different
and sometimes the same.

1. Listen and point to the matching pictures.

2. How are you today?

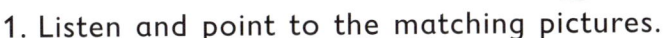

Girl and boy scouts

„Jeden Tag eine gute Tat." ist das Motto der Pfadfinder. Wusstet ihr eigentlich, dass die Pfadfinder ihren Ursprung in England haben? Dort heißen die Pfadfinder *scouts*. Es gibt Mädchengruppen (*girl scouts*) und Jungengruppen (*boy scouts*). Ein Pfadfinder, egal ob in England oder in Deutschland, beachtet immer bestimmte Regeln:

– er hilft anderen, wenn er kann (*helping others*),

– er versucht, immer höflich zu sein (*being polite*),

– er teilt mit anderen (*sharing*).

 Einen Text hören und verstehen.
Über Befinden und Gefühle sprechen.
Landeskundliche Informationen über Pfadfinder erhalten.

nine   9

Welcome to Paddington Zoo

polar bears

FEEDING TIMES & SHOWS

11.00 a.m. dolphin show

11.30 a.m. pelicans

11.50 a.m. giant tortoises

12.15 p.m. tigers and lions
and keeper talk

2.00 p.m. seal show

3.15 p.m. monkeys
and keeper talk

TICKETS	PRICE
adult (16–99 years)	£13.90
child (3–15 years)	£10.90
under 3's	free

Gift Shop

Kiosk

crocodiles

kangaroos

parrots

£3.50

£3.50

ICE CREAM

£3.50

penguins

Into Africa:
giraffes & zebras

1. Talk about the picture.

2. Find out about the feeding times and shows.

3. What do the people want to do at the zoo? Listen.

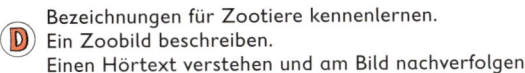

Bezeichnungen für Zootiere kennenlernen.
Ⓓ Ein Zoobild beschreiben.
Einen Hörtext verstehen und am Bild nachverfolgen.

At a dolphin show

Dolphins can dive deep.
They can swim very fast.

They can dance.

They can sing.

What can dolphins do?

They can do tricks.

 1. Listen and point.

 2. What do YOU know about dolphins?

 2. Get more information on the Internet.

Einen Hörtext verstehen.
D Über Delfine sprechen.

This dolphin can play ball.

Dolphins can jump high.

Dolphin *(Cetacea)*

Height:	3–4,2 metres (10–14 feet)
Weight:	160–270 kilograms (350–600 pounds)
Food:	fish, shrimp and squid
Where it lives:	all over the world; temperate coastal waters
Number of young:	1
Lifespan:	25–30 years
Other facts:	Dolphins are very intelligent. They communicate by sound, clicking and whistling.

They can do tricks.

Animals around the world

Pandas
Pandas live in China.
They are black and white.
They have big bodies
but small ears.
Pandas eat bamboo leaves.
They can climb.

 1. Read the panda profile.

 2. Talk about your favourite animal.

 3. Write a profile of an animal.

Young Panda

Der WWF (*World Wide Fund of Nature*) ist
eine der größten Naturschutzorganisationen der Welt. Im Kinder- und
Jugendclub, dem *Young Panda,* erfahren Kinder und Jugendliche alles,
was sie über Tiere und Natur wissen wollen. Auf dem Logo des WWF
sieht man den Großen Panda oder Bambusbär. Er gehört zu den
bedrohtesten Tierarten der Welt. („Bedrohte Tiere" heißt auf Englisch
übrigens *endangered animals*.) Die etwa 1.600 noch in der Wildnis
lebenden Pandas verteilen sich auf sechs Bergregionen im Südwesten
Chinas. Mehr Informationen kannst du auch im Internet finden.

 Einen Text über Pandas lesen und verstehen.
Über Tiere / das eigene Lieblingstier sprechen und schreiben.
Informationen über eine Naturschutzorganisation erhalten.

The zoo is lots of fun!

Let's begin with one:
the zoo is lots of fun.

One and two,
see a kangaroo.

Two and three,
see a chimpanzee.

Three and four,
hear the lions roar.

Four and five,
watch the dolphins dive.

Five and six,
there's a monkey doing tricks.

Six and seven,
the parrot is eleven.

Seven and eight,
a tiger and his mate.

Eight and nine,
penguins in a line.

Nine and ten,
I want to come again!

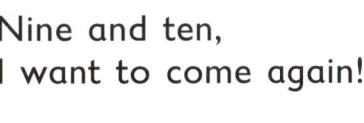

I'm eleven

1. Find the matching pictures.

2. Get into animal groups. Act it out!

Ein Gedicht verstehen.
Ein Rollenspiel durchführen.

When I grow up

A policewoman **METROPOLITAN POLICE** Working together for a safer London

I'm a policewoman
dressed in blue.
If you have a problem,
I'll help you.
Call me on the phone
on 9-9-9.
I'll come quickly
and that is fine!

When I grow up
I want to be a policewoman.

doctor

hairdresser

 1. Read the poem.

 2. Listen and find the matching pictures.

 3. Play a miming game.

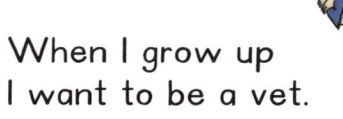

When I grow up
I want to be a vet.

Ein Gedicht lesen lernen.
Berufsbezeichnungen kennenlernen.
Berufe pantomimisch darstellen.

shop assistant

baker

postman

vet

What does a pilot do?

A firefighter puts out fires and saves people.

Wow, when I grow up I want to be a firefighter.

teacher

My dad is a baker

1.

2.

3.

4.

5.

6.

a) Mr Curtis takes the fresh bread out of the forms.

b) Before he finishes work he cleans the bakery.

c) Mr Curtis starts work at 3 o'clock in the morning. First he mixes the dough.

d) Mr Curtis goes home at lunchtime.

e) Then he kneads the dough. He bakes bread, rolls and cakes.

f) He brings the bread, rolls and cakes into the shop.

 1. What does a baker do? Listen.

 2. Look at the pictures and find the matching sentences.

 3. Listen and find the mistakes.

Tätigkeitsablauf eines Bäckers kennenlernen.

Jump rope rhyme

Early in the morning at half past eight

I heard the milkman knocking at the gate,

up jumps (player's name) to open the door.

How many bottles are on the floor?

One, two, three, four, five ...

1. Read the rhyme and learn it by heart.

Milkman

Den traditionellen Beruf des *milkman* wird es in Großbritannien bald nicht mehr geben. Noch vor wenigen Jahren fuhr der *milkman* früh morgens im Elektroauto seine Runden.

Er stellte die bestellten Milchflaschen vor fast jede Haustür und sammelte am Ende der Woche das *milkmoney* ein. Heute kaufen die meisten Leite ihre Milch im Tetrapack im Supermarkt.

Einen Kinderreim lesen und auswendig lernen.
Landeskundliche Informationen über den traditionellen Beruf des *milkman* erhalten.

The weather

snowy

foggy

stormy

Can we go to the forest on Thursday?

On Thursday it will be sunny and warm.

cloudy

hot

calm

sunny

cold

frosty

Weather forecast for London, UK		9 a.m.	4 p.m.
Monday, 6th September	cloudy	10°C	17°C
Tuesday, 7th September	rainy	9°C	16°C
Wednesday, 8th September	rainy & stormy	9°C	15°C
Thursday, 9th September	sunny	12°C	19°C
Friday, 10th September	cloudy	10°C	17°C

windy

warm

rainy

1. Make the weather forecast for London.

2. Look out of the window. What's the weather like today?

Eine Wettervorhersage verstehen.
Über das Wetter sprechen.

Experience nature

1. Listen and point.

2. What can you hear, see, smell, taste or feel in the forest?

Sinneswahrnehmungen kennenlernen und darüber sprechen.

Nature book

Rain
Rain on the green grass.
Rain on the tree.
Rain on the flower.
But not on me!

Sun
Sun on the green grass.
Sun on the tree.
Sun on the flower.
And please on me!

17

1. Listen and learn the nature rhymes by heart.

2. Create your own nature book.

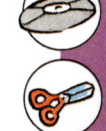

 Naturgedichte verstehen und auswendig lernen.
Ein eigenes *nature book* erstellen.

Recycling

Put the plastic bottle into the plastic container.

Recycling in England

Wisst ihr eigentlich, dass das Wort *Recycling* aus dem Englischen kommt? Es bedeutet, dass man etwas wiederverwendet. Genau wie in Deutschland wird in englischen Schulen der Müll getrennt. Die Container sehen fast so aus wie bei uns:

 1. What do you put into the containers?

Über Mülltrennung sprechen.
Landeskundliche Informationen über Mülltrennung erhalten.

Tips for kids

 1. Collect glass, paper, cans
and plastic.

 2. Don't use plastic bags.
Use a cloth bag.

3. Save paper.
Use both sides of the sheet.

4. Don't throw away your litter.
Put it into a bin.

5. Collect your batteries.

6. Save energy. Switch off
the light, computer, radio or TV.

1. Read the text and talk about it.

2. What else can you do to save nature?

(D) Tipps für mehr Umweltbewusstsein verstehen und darüber sprechen.

Native Americans

feather

bear

shield

canoe

berries

drum

eagle

1. What can you see in the picture?

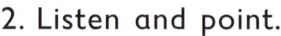

2. Listen and point.

D Einzelne Begriffe benennen.
Informationen über *Native Americans* erhalten.

axe

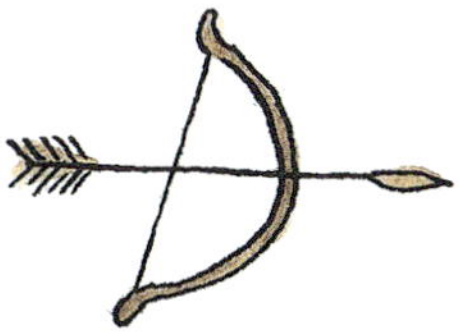

bow and arrow

peace pipe

moccasins

Chief Sitting Bull

The first settlers

Pocahontas

corn

wigwam

totem pole

buffalo hide

buffalo

beaver

elk

twenty-seven

Pocahontas

Many years ago English people sailed to America
and settled there.
They met Native Americans.
One of them was Pocahontas.
The settlers and the Native Americans
were not always good friends.
They had fights over land and food.

Pocahontas liked the settlers.
She visited them and learned their language.
One day Pocahontas came to her village
and saw one of the settlers bound to a tree.
His name was John Smith.

Die Legende von Pocahontas kennenlernen.
D   Eine Legende verstehen und nacherzählen.

Pocahontas was shocked.
Her father, Chief Powhatan,
wanted to kill John Smith.
Pocahontas begged for the settler's life.
Chief Powhatan gave in
because he loved his daughter.
John Smith was saved.

1. Listen to the legend and tell it in German.

Native Americans

Als Christoph Kolumbus Amerika entdeckte,
glaubte er, er sein in Indien. Er hielt daher
die Ureinwohner für *Indians*. An der Ostküste
lebten damals die sesshaften *Native Americans*. Sie wohnten in *wigwam*-
Dörfern. Andere Stämme lebten in den *Great Plains*. Sie zogen ihrem
Jagdwild, dem *buffalo*, hinterher und wohnten in Zelten, die sie *tipis*
nannten. Eine berühmte Indianerin war Pocahontas.
Sie soll als Kind dem weißen Kapitän John Smith das
Leben gerettet haben. Im Jahr 1614 heiratete Pocahontas
einen englischen Siedler. Wenig später reiste sie mit ihm
nach England. Dort wurde sie sogar dem König vorgestellt.
In ihre Heimat kehrte Pocahontas nie zurück. Sie starb
auf der Heimreise an einer Lungenentzündung.

Landeskundliche Informationen über *Native Americans* erhalten.

Homes

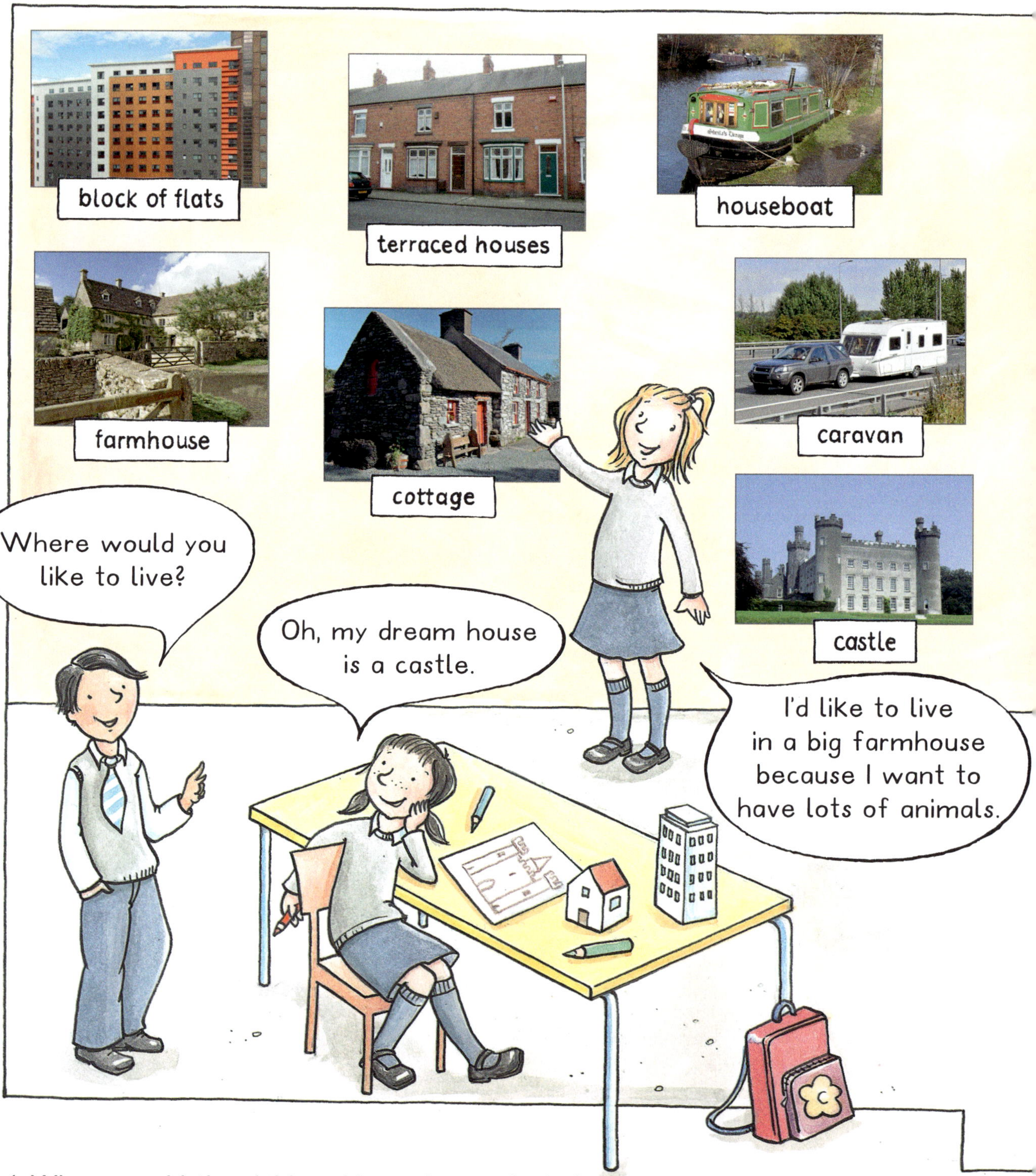

block of flats

terraced houses

houseboat

farmhouse

cottage

caravan

castle

Where would you like to live?

Oh, my dream house is a castle.

I'd like to live in a big farmhouse because I want to have lots of animals.

 1. Where would the children like to live and why?

 2. Where would you like to live?

Verschiedene Möglichkeiten zum Wohnen kennenlernen.
(D) Vorlieben für ein eigenes Zuhause äußern.

Our house

attic

parents' bedroom

bathroom

my bedroom

kitchen

living room

cellar

Our flat

1 hall   4 bedroom
2 living room   5 kitchen
3 bedroom   6 bathroom
              7 balcony

Has your flat got a balcony?

No, it hasn't.
It has got a terrace.

I live in a block of flats.
Our flat has got five rooms.
It has got a balcony.

1. Listen and describe Ben's flat.

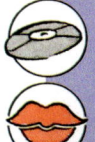

thirty-one   31

Emma's new home

1. Listen. Where do they take the furniture?

2. Listen to the new neighbours.

Einrichtungs- und Gebrauchsgegenstände kennenlernen.

I love my home

I live in a flat
high up there.
Where the sun shines in,
up in the air.

There are lifts and stairs,
and ten floors.
There are balconies too,
and windows and doors.

Our flat is just right,
not too big, not too small.
We have got four rooms
plus a kitchen and hall.

I like to live here.
It really is fun.
I am very near
to the moon and the sun!

1. Read the poem and learn it by heart.

Door knockers

In England gibt es viele alte Haustüren. Sie sind oft
leuchtend rot oder schwarz lackiert. Auf den meisten
Haustüren prangt ein *door knocker*. Das sind Türklopfer
aus Metall. Man kann Pferdeköpfe, Löwen oder Hunde auf
den Türen finden. Früher klopften Besucher
damit an die Tür. Heute sind sie nur noch
Zierde und werden liebevoll geputzt, mit *elbow grease*.
Wörtlich übersetzt heißt das Ellenbogenschmalz, hier ist
aber gemeint: mit viel Kraft in den Armen. Jedenfalls
glänzen die *door knockers* danach gold oder silber.

D Ein Gedicht lesen und auswendig lernen.
Landeskundliche Informationen über die Gestaltung der Haustüren erhalten.

thirty-three   33

Mum's house, Dad's flat

Hello, I'm Cathy. I live in a house and I live in a flat.

I like to be with Mum in her house.

I like to be with Dad in his flat.

I've got a bedroom at Mum's house.

I've got a bedroom at Dad's flat.

1. Listen to the story.

2. Cathy likes to be with her Mum AND her Dad. Why?

3. Write about your home or make a poster.

4. Present your text or your poster.

D Eine Geschichte verstehen und Fragen dazu beantworten.
D Das eigene Zuhause beschreiben.

thirty-five

The Gingerbread Man

1. Listen and follow the story.

2. Read the texts.

3. Do a role play. Think of more animals.

 Ein englisches *Traditional* kennenlernen.
Eine Geschichte weiterführen und in ein Rollenspiel umsetzen.

Jack and the beanstalk

Once upon a time there was a 🧒 called Jack.

He lived with his 👩. They had no 💰.

One day Jack's 👩 said, "We must sell our 🐄. Take it to the market."

On his way to the market Jack met a 🤴.

The 🤴 gave Jack **5** magic 🫘 for the 🐄.

Jack's 👩 was very angry.

She threw the 🫘 out of the 🪟.

The next morning, there was a huge 🌱 in front of the 🪟.

Jack climbed up the 🌱. He climbed higher and higher.

When he was on top, Jack saw a beautiful 🏰. He went inside.

A voice shouted loudly,

"Fee, fi, fo, fum — I smell the blood of an Englishman!"

Jack was scared and jumped into a 🗄️.

Jack saw an enormous 🧍 coming into the kitchen. The 🧍

was standing in front of a 🐔. The 🐔 laid an 🥚.

It was made of 🪙. — Wow! A magic 🐔!

When the 🧍 was sleeping, Jack jumped out of the 🗄️.

He took the 🐔 and started to run.

Ⓓ   Ein traditionelles englisches Märchen kennenlernen.
Ein Märchen gestaltend (laut) vorlesen.

Suddenly the 🧔 woke up. He shouted,

"Fee, fi, fo, fum – I smell the blood an Englishman!

Here I come!"

Jack ran faster. He climbed down the 🌱. The 🧔 climbed after him.

Jack shouted, "👩! Help!" Jack's 👩 took an 🪓

and chopped down the 🌱. The 🧔 fell and crashed to the ground.

Nobody ever saw him again. And Jack and his 👩?

They lived happily ever after –

and the magic 🐔 laid many 🥚 made of 🟨.

1. Listen to the story and tell it in German.

2. Read along and speak the picture words.

Fairy tales

Viele Märchen, die es in England gibt, kennen wir auch in Deutschland. Das liegt daran, dass sie einen gemeinsamen Ursprung haben. Manche Märchen werden überall in Europa in jeder Landessprache erzählt. *Fairy tales*, die englische Kinder genauso lesen wie deutsche Kinder, sind zum Beispiel *Hansel and Gretel, Cinderella, Little Red Riding Hood* oder *Rumpelstiltskin*. Ursprüngliche englische Märchen gibt es aber auch. Sie heißen *Jack and the beanstalk, Goldilocks and the three bears, The three little pigs* und *The Gingerbread Man*.

The three little pigs

Jack and the beanstalk

The Gingerbread Man

Goldilocks and the three bears

Landeskundliche Informationen über Märchen erhalten.

thirty-nine

The fox and the crow

One day a crow
found some cheese.
She was very happy.

The crow flew onto a tree.
There she wanted to eat
the cheese.

On his way home, Master Fox
came out of the forest.
He was very hungry.

When he saw the crow
with the cheese
he had an idea.

He sat down under the tree
and started to talk to the crow.
"Hello, Miss Crow.
Can you sing for me, please?"

The crow started to sing.
But – she lost the cheese!
It fell to the ground.

MORAL:

Do not trust people
who talk sweet to you.

Master Fox caught the cheese.
He looked up to the crow and
smiled, "You are a stupid crow."

1. Read the story and tell it in German. Do you understand the moral?

2. Act it out.

 Eine Fabel verstehen und auf Deutsch nacherzählen.
Die Fabel in ein Rollenspiel umsetzen.

A weekend in London

boat

plane

scooter

I walk

> We can all go by underground.

> Let's take a doubledecker bus!

car

bike

underground

train

taxi

How about walking?

Hello Emma,
Hooray, we are coming!
I'm so happy.
We are staying
from Friday to Sunday.
See you soon.
Your penfriend
Anna

1. Listen to the CD.

2. What are their plans?

doubledecker bus

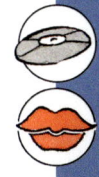

Einem Hörtext Informationen entnehmen.
Über Pläne sprechen.

(D)

London sights

The Tower of London
is an old castle.

Tower Bridge is a big draw bridge
over the river Thames.

London Eye is
the biggest Ferris Wheel
in Europe.

The sound of Big Ben
is very famous.

Horse Guards

Westminster Abbey
is a big and famous church.

The Queen lives in
Buckingham Palace.

Lord Nelson

Nelson's Column is in
Trafalgar Square.

We have a big church
in Essen, too.

LONDON SIGHTSEEING

1. Listen to the tour and point to the matching pictures.

2. What is your town famous for?

3. Listen to the sounds of London.

 Sehenswürdigkeiten von London kennenlernen.
D Über Sehenswürdigkeiten der Heimatstadt sprechen.

forty-five   45

A map of London

Horse Guards

National Gallery

Nelson's Column in Trafalgar Square

Bruton St.

Piccadilly

Regent Street

St. James's Street

Pall

Mall East

Charing Cross Road

The Strand

Lancaster Place

Waterloo Bridge

Embankment

The Mall

Horse Guard's Road

Whitehall

Victoria

Thames

You are here.

Buckingham Palace

Birdcage Walk

Parliament Square

Westminster Bridge

Thames Path

York Rd.

Hobart Place

Palace Road

Victoria Street

Buckingham Gate

Buckingham

Parliament Street

River

Lambeth Palace Rd.

Westminster Abbey

Big Ben

Lambeth Bridge

London Eye

 1. Listen and follow the directions.

Einer Beschreibung folgen.

Directions

turn left

turn right

go straight on

on the left

on the right

Excuse me,
how can I get to
Big Ben?

Go straight on,
then turn left.
Big Ben is on the right.

1. Ask the way. Work with a partner.

The London underground

In London gibt es die älteste U-Bahn der Welt. Sie wurde 1863 eröffnet. Die Londoner nennen ihre U-Bahn *Tube*. Manche Linien liegen 20m unter der Erdoberfläche. Viele steile *escalators* führen zu diesen Linien hinunter.
Diese wichtige Regel sollte man auf der Rolltreppe unbedingt beachten: *Stand on the right*. So kommen die Fahrgäste, die es besonders eilig haben, gut an den anderen vorbei. Wer sich an diese Regel nicht hält, macht sich bei den Londonern sehr unbeliebt.

Ⓓ Eine Wegbeschreibung formulieren und verstehen.
Landeskundliche Informationen über die U-Bahn in London erhalten.

In the park

D Personen, Tiere und Handlungen beschreiben.

1. Describe the picture.

2. Listen and find the matching people.

3. Do a role play.

Verschiedene Dialoge den passenden Situationen zuordnen.
Verschiedene Rollenspiele durchführen.

What happens on the pond?

1. **2.**

3. **4.**

5. **6.** ?

Father duck attacks the boat. The boat drifts off.

The boy plays with his boat.

A duck family swims on the pond. There are five little ducklings.

The stick is too short.

The dog …

A boy and his dog help.

 1. Listen to the story.

 2. Look at the pictures and find the matching sentences.

 3. What happens in picture 6?

Eine Geschichte verstehen und vervollständigen.
(D) Die Geschichte auf Englisch nacherzählen.

Ice cream

In the summer
when it's sunny,
eating ice cream is so funny.

I love ice cream
in a cone
with many tasty scoops, says Joan.

It's so lovely
sweet and licky,
but when it drips, you will get sticky.

I get ice cream
on my clothes,
in my hair and on my nose.

My mum says,
please lick fast,
or this ice cream will be your last!

STRAWBERRY
VANILLA
AFTER EIGHT
COCONUT
BANANA
CHOCOLATE
CHERRY
LEMON

1. Listen to the poem.

2. Read along and learn the poem by heart.

3. What are your favourite ice cream flavours?

Ice cream

In England findet man bei schönem Wetter in vielen Parks einen *ice cream van*. Man bekommt das Eis als Kugel (*scoop*) in einer Waffeltüte (*cone*). Einige Eiswagen bieten auch Softeis an, das auf Wunsch nicht nur Sirup als *topping* erhält, sondern zusätzlich in süße Zucker- oder Schokoladenstreusel (*sprinkles*) gedreht wird. Als Krönung erhält das Eis einen *chocolate flake,* das ist eine dünne gedrehte Schokoladenstange.

Ein Gedicht lesen und verstehen.
Landeskundliche Informationen zum Eisessen in England erhalten.

A sandwich, please!

1. What would you like on your sandwich?

2. Do a role play.

Sandwichzutaten kennenlernen.
D Dialog in ein Rollenspiel umsetzen.

Mini pizzas

ROLLS · RED PEPPER · TOMATO KETCHUP · TUNA · BAKING TRAY · TOMATOES · CHEESE · PEPPERONI · HAM · OLIVES · 180°C/356°F · OVEN

Cut the rolls in half.

Put some tomato ketchup on the rolls.

Choose your favourite toppings.
Add the cheese.

Put the rolls on the baking tray.
Cook them for ten minutes in
the oven.
The pizzas are ready – enjoy!

1. Read the instructions and find the matching pictures.

2. Try it out!

Schriftliche Anweisungen lesen und verstehen.
Gemeinsam Minipizzen backen.

The first Thanksgiving

1. Listen to the story about the first Thanksgiving.

Den historischen Hintergrund von *Thanksgiving* kennenlernen.

Celebrating Thanksgiving

Thanksgiving is a holiday in the USA.
It is on the fourth Thursday in November.
People celebrate the first Thanksgiving.
They send cards.

Families get together.
Sons, daughters, grandparents,
uncles, aunts and cousins come home.
The traditional food is turkey,
potatoes, pumpkin and corn.

There is a big Thanksgiving parade
in New York.

In the afternoon, most families
watch American football on TV.

1. Read the texts.

2. How do people celebrate Thanksgiving?

Landeskundliche Informationen zu *Thanksgiving* erhalten.

The farmer's Christmas

The farmer and his wife are very hungry. They want to have dinner.

Suddenly there is a knock at the door.

We are Mary and Joseph. Where can we sleep? – I don't have a room. But there is a stable in the fields.

The farmer and his wife sit down again. They want to have dinner.

But there is a knock at the door.

We are the three shepherds. Where are Mary and Joseph? – Mary and Joseph? Have a look in the stable in the fields.

The farmer and his wife sit down again. They want to have dinner.

But there is a knock at the door.

We are the three kings.
Where are Mary and Joseph? –
In the stable in the fields.

The farmer and his wife sit down again. They are angry.
Now they want to have dinner.

Suddenly there is an angel at the door.

Now the farmer and his wife are not angry any longer.
They are happy.

1. Listen to the story.

2. Do a role play.

Eine Weihnachtsgeschichte kennenlernen.
Geschichte in ein Rollenspiel umsetzen.

Fit for 5!

Bumblebee card

⚀ Say out loud 5 words.   ⚁ Ask a question.   ⚂ Talk about the picture.

⚃ Make a roleplay.   ⚄ Make a riddle.   ⚅ Take a card.

1. Play the game.

Look it up

A

afternoon .... der Nachmittag

angry .... wütend

answer .... die Antwort
antworten

arm .... der Arm

armchair .... der Sessel

attic .... der Dachboden

aunt .... die Tante

autumn .... der Herbst

B

back .... der Rücken
zurück

bake .... backen

baker .... die Bäckerin, der Bäcker

bakery .... die Bäckerei

baking tray .... das Backblech

balcony .... der Balkon

ball .... der Ball

bathroom .... das Badezimmer

bear .... der Bär

beautiful .... schön

beaver .... der Biber

bed .... das Bett

bedroom .... das Schlafzimmer

behind .... hinter

big .... groß

bin .... der Papierkorb

bird .... der Vogel

black .... schwarz

blue .... blau

boat .... das Boot

bonfire .... das Lagerfeuer

book .... das Buch

bookshelf .... das Bücherregal

boots .... die Stiefel

bottle .... die Flasche

bread .... das Brot

brother .... der Bruder

brown .... braun

buffalo .... der Büffel

build .... bauen

bumblebee .... die Hummel

bus .... der Bus

bush .... der Busch

C

cake .... der Kuchen

call .... anrufen

cap .... das Cap

carpet .... der Teppich

castle .... das Schloss

catch .... fangen

cellar .... der Keller

chair .... der Stuhl

cheese .... der Käse

chess .... das Schachspiel

chicken .... das Huhn, das Hühnchen

child .... das Kind

children .... die Kinder

chips .... die Pommes frites

choose .... aussuchen

Christmas .... Weihnachten

church .... die Kirche

clock .... die Uhr

clothes .... die Kleidung

coast .... die Küste

coffee .... der Kaffee

collect .... sammeln

colour .... die Farbe
anmalen

come from .... herkommen

cook .... kochen

cooker .... der Herd

country .... das Land

cousin .... die Cousine, der Cousin

crazy .... verrückt

cricket	das Cricket(-spiel)
crisps	die Chips
crocodile	das Krokodil
cucumber	die Gurke
cupboard	der (Küchen.)Schrank
cut	schneiden
cycling	das Fahrradfahren

D

dance	tanzen
dark	dunkel
daughter	die Tochter
day	der Tag
deep	tief
describe	beschreiben
dinner	das Abendessen
dive	tauchen
doctor	die Ärztin, der Arzt
dog	der Hund
dolphin	der Delphin
door	die Tür
do tricks	Kunststücke machen
draw	malen
dress	das Kleid
get dressed	anziehen
duck	die Ente
duckling	das Entenküken

E

ear	das Ohr
eat	essen
elephant	der Elefant
engineer	die Ingenieurin, der Ingenieur
evening	der Abend
evil	böse

F

famous	bekannt
farmer	die Bäuerin, der Bauer
farmhouse	der Bauernhof
fast	schnell
father / dad	der Vater / der Papa
favourite	Lieblings-
feed	füttern
feel	fühlen
find	finden
fire	das Feuer
firefighter	die Feuerwehrfrau der Feuerwehrmann
fireworks	das Feuerwerk
fish	der Fisch
flat	die Wohnung
flower	die Blume
fly	fliegen
follow	folgen
football	Fußball
forest	der Wald
fox	der Fuchs
free	frei
Friday	der Freitag
fridge	der Kühlschrank
friend	die Freundin, der Freund
frog	der Frosch

G

game	das Spiel
gardening	die Gartenarbeit
giraffe	die Giraffe
girl	das Mädchen
give	geben
glad	zufrieden, froh
glass	das Glas
glove	der Handschuh
go	gehen
go by bike	Fahrrad fahren
go home	nach Hause gehen
go shopping	einkaufen gehen

Look it up

good .... gut
grandfather .... der Großvater
grandpa .... der Opa
grandmother ..... die Großmutter
grandma .... die Oma
grapes .... die Weintrauben
grass .... das Gras

H

hair .... das Haar
hairdresser .... die Friseurin, der Friseur
hall .... der Flur
ham .... der Schinken
happy .... glücklich
has (got) .... hat
have (got) .... haben
head .... der Kopf
hear .... hören
heart .... das Herz
hedgehog .... der Igel
help .... helfen
holiday .... die Ferien
home .... das Zuhause
horse .... das Pferd
house .... das Haus
houseboat .... das Hausboot
hungry .... hungrig
husband .... der Ehemann

I

ice cream .... das Eis
ill .... krank
in .... in
in front of .... vor

J

juice .... der Saft
jump .... springen

K

kangaroo .... das Känguru
king .... der König
kitchen .... die Küche
knee .... das Knie
knife .... das Messer

L

label .... beschriften
lamp .... die Lampe
lazy .... faul
learn .... lernen
left .... links
leg .... das Bein
letter .... der Brief
lettuce .... der Salat
life .... das Leben
light .... das Licht
                          hell-
like .... mögen
don't like .... nicht mögen
lion .... der Löwe
listen (to) .... zuhören
live .... leben
living room .... das Wohnzimmer
look up .... nachschlagen

M

man .... der Mann
matching .... passend
minute .... die Minute
mirror .... der Spiegel
mistake .... der Fehler
Monday .... der Montag
monkey .... der Affe
moon .... der Mond
morning .... der Morgen
mother / mum .... die Mutter / die Mama
mouth .... der Mund

N

name .... der Name
naughty .... ungezogen
next to .... neben
night .... die Nacht
nose .... die Nase
nurse .... die Krankenschwester

O

old .... alt
on .... auf
order .... bestellen
oven .... der Ofen

P

paint .... malen
painting .... das Gemälde
                              das Malen
pancake .... der Pfannkuchen
panda .... der Panda
paper .... das Papier
parents .... die Eltern
park .... der Park
parrot .... der Papagei
penfriend .... die Brieffreundin
                              der Brieffreund
penguin .... der Pinguin
pepperoni .... die Salami
picture .... das Bild
pilot .... die Pilotin, der Pilot
plane .... das Flugzeug
plate .... der Teller
play .... spielen
point (to) .... zeigen
polar bear .... der Eisbär
policeman .... der Polizist
policewoman ..... die Polizistin
pond .... der Teich
poor .... arm

postman .... der Postbote
potato .... die Kartoffel
prince .... der Prinz

Qu

queen .... die Königin
quick .... schnell

R

radio .... das Radio
rain .... der Regen
                              regnen
read .... lesen
recorder .... die Blockflöte
remember .... erinnern
ride .... reiten
right .... rechts
                              richtig
river .... der Fluss
role play .... das Rollenspiel
roll .... das Brötchen
room .... das Zimmer
run .... laufen, rennen

S

sad .... traurig
sailing .... das Segeln
sandwich .... das Butterbrot
Saturday .... der Samstag
say .... sagen
school .... die Schule
school uniform ... die Schuluniform
see .... sehen
sheep .... das Schaf, die Schafe
shield .... das Schild
ship .... das Schiff
shoe .... der Schuh
shop assistant ... die Verkäuferin
                              der Verkäufer

Look it up

sing .... singen
sit .... sitzen
skiing .... das Skifahren
sleep .... schlafen
smell .... riechen
snake .... die Schlange
son .... der Sohn
song .... das Lied
speak .... sprechen
spring .... der Frühling
stable .... der Stall
stair .... die Treppe
star .... der Stern
stay .... bleiben
stepmother .... die Stiefmutter
stop .... aufhören
summer .... der Sommer
sun .... die Sonne
Sunday .... der Sonntag
sweet .... süß
sweets .... die Süßigkeiten
swim .... schwimmen

T

tail .... der Schwanz
talk .... sprechen
taste .... schmecken
tea .... der Tee
teacher .... die Lehrerin, der Lehrer
tell .... erzählen
terraced house .. das Reihenhaus
Thursday .... der Donnerstag
tiger .... der Tiger
tired .... müde
today .... heute
tomato .... die Tomate
town .... die Stadt
travel .... reisen
treasure .... der Schatz

tree .... der Baum
Tuesday .... der Dienstag
tuna .... der Thunfisch
turkey .... der Truthahn
TV .... der Fernseher

U

uncle .... der Onkel
under .... unter
underground ...... die U-Bahn

V

vet .... die Tierärztin, der Tierarzt
violin .... die Geige

W

walk .... gehen
water .... das Wasser
wardrobe .... der (Kleider)Schrank
weather .... das Wetter
weather forecast die Wettervorhersage
Wednesday .... der Mittwoch
weekend .... das Wochenende
wife .... die Ehefrau
window .... das Fenster
winter .... der Winter
woman .... die Frau
work .... die Arbeit
                          arbeiten
world .... die Welt
write .... schreiben
wrong .... falsch

X
Y

year .... das Jahr
yesterday .... gestern

Z

zebra .... das Zebra
zoo .... der Zoo